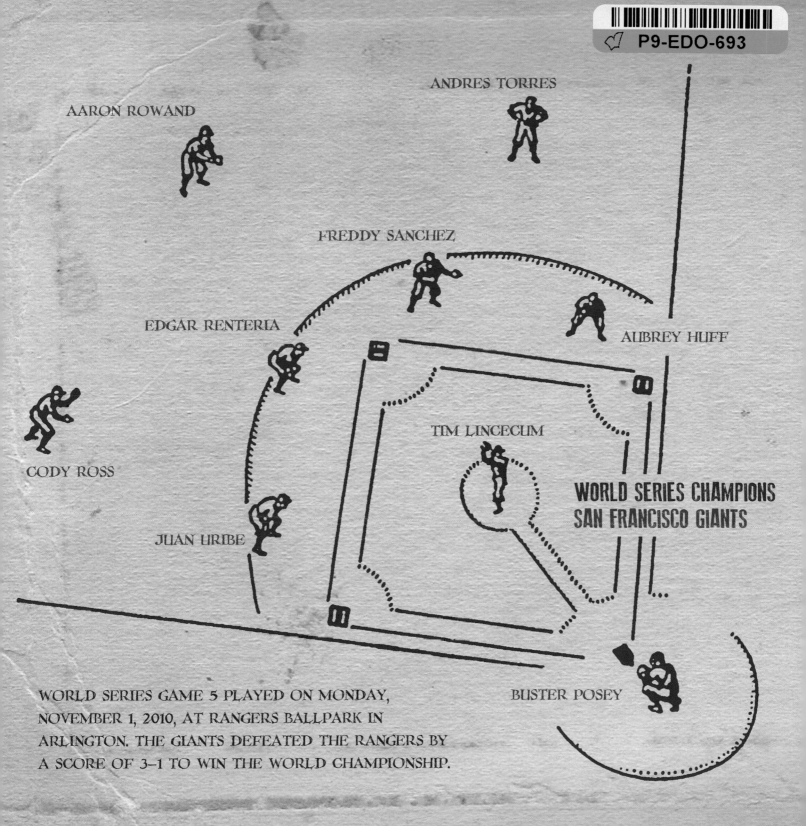

WORLD SERIES GAME 5 PLAYED ON MONDAY, NOVEMBER 1, 2010, AT RANGERS BALLPARK IN ARLINGTON. THE GIANTS DEFEATED THE RANGERS BY A SCORE OF 3–1 TO WIN THE WORLD CHAMPIONSHIP.

WORLD SERIES CHAMPIONS

SAN FRANCISCO GIANTS

SARA GILBERT

CREATIVE
PAPERBACKS

Published by Creative Paperbacks
P.O. Box 227, Mankato, Minnesota 56002
Creative Paperbacks is an imprint of The Creative Company
www.thecreativecompany.us

Design and production by Blue Design (www.bluedes.com)
Art direction by Rita Marshall
Printed in the United States of America

Photographs by AP Images, Getty Images (APA, Robert Beck/
Sports Illustrated, Chicago History Museum, Monica Davey/
AFP, Diamond Images, Dennis Desprois/MLB Photos, Mitchell
Funk, Jeff Haynes/AFP, Thearon W. Henderson, Jed Jacobsohn,
Paul Kitagaki Jr./Sacramento Bee/MCT, Mitchell Layton, Brad
Mangin/MLB Photos, Peter Read Miller/Sports Illustrated, MLB
Photos, National Baseball Hall of Fame Library/MLB Photos, Olen
Collection/Diamond Images, Photo File, Rich Pilling/MLB Photos,
Mark Rucker/Transcendental Graphics, Don Smith/MLB Photos,
Justin Sullivan, Al Tielemans/Sports Illustrated, Tony Tomsic/
WireImage, Ron Vesely/MLB Photos)

Library of Congress Cataloging-in-Publication Data
Gilbert, Sara.
San Francisco Giants / Sara Gilbert.
p. cm. — (World series champions)
Includes bibliographical references and index.
Summary: A simple introduction to the San Francisco Giants major
league baseball team, including its start in 1883 in New York, its
World Series triumphs, and its stars throughout the years.
ISBN 978-1-60818-272-5 (hardcover)
ISBN 978-0-89812-823-9 (pbk)
1. San Francisco Giants (Baseball team)—History—Juvenile
literature. I. Title.
GV875.S34G55 2013
796.357'640979461—dc23   2012004266

First edition
9 8 7 6 5 4 3 2 1

Cover: Catcher Buster Posey
Page 2: Pitcher Madison Bumgarner
Page 3: Pitcher Matt Cain
Right: New York's Polo Grounds (1895)

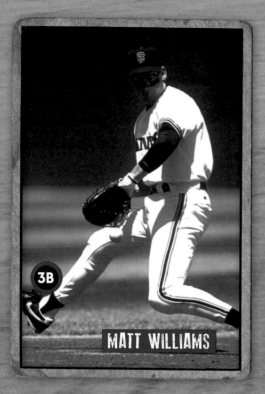

3B

MATT WILLIAMS

3B

JIM DAVENPORT

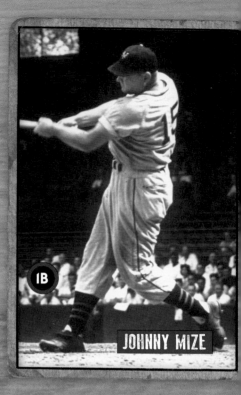

1B

JOHNNY MIZE

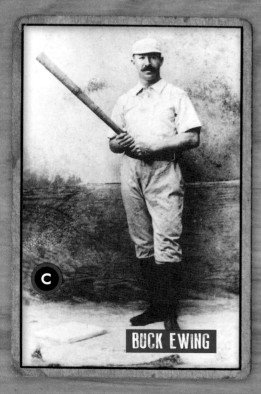

C

BUCK EWING

1B

J. T. SNOW

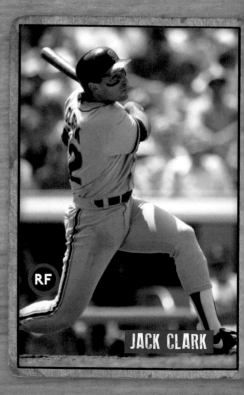

RF

JACK CLARK

TABLE OF CONTENTS

SAN FRANCISCO AND AT&T PARK 9

RIVALS AND COLORS 10

GIANTS HISTORY 12

GIANTS STARS 19

HOW THE GIANTS GOT THEIR NAME 23

ABOUT THE GIANTS 23

GLOSSARY 24

INDEX .24

SAN FRANCISCO AND AT&T PARK

San Francisco is a city in California next to the Pacific Ocean. It is the home of the famous Golden Gate Bridge. San Francisco is also the home of AT&T Park. That is where a major league baseball team called the Giants plays.

RIVALS AND COLORS

The Giants play against 29 other major-league teams to try to win the World Series and become world champions. The Giants wear black, orange, and white uniforms. Their main **RIVALS** are the Los Angeles Dodgers.

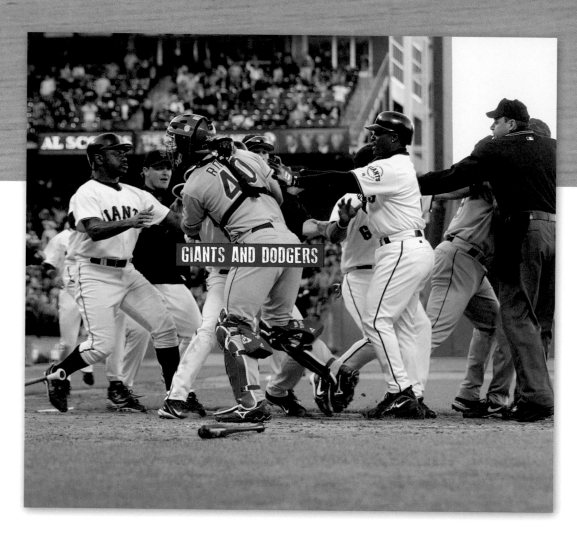

GIANTS AND DODGERS

PITCHER JUAN MARICHAL

GIANTS HISTORY

The Giants' first season was in 1883. They played in New York then and were called the Gothams. In 1885, they became the Giants. The Giants got to the World Series in 1905 and beat the Philadelphia Athletics easily.

Hard-throwing pitcher Christy Mathewson helped

THIRD BASEMAN BOBBY THOMSON

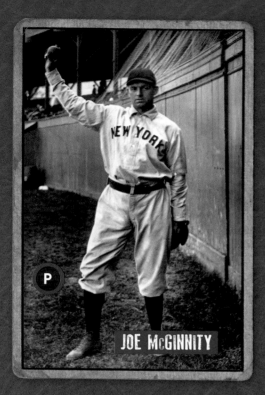

P

JOE McGINNITY

1B

FRED MERKLE

RF

BOBBY BONDS

1B

WILL CLARK

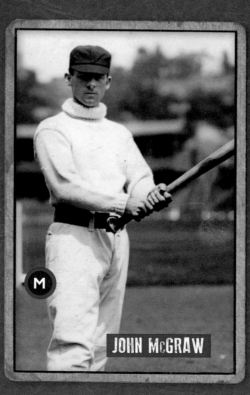

M

JOHN McGRAW

3B

DARRELL EVANS

MEL OTT

the Giants reach the World Series 8 times over the next 20 years. They won in 1921 and 1922. The Giants beat their **CROSSTOWN** rivals, the New York Yankees, both times.

Stars like right fielder Mel Ott helped the Giants win many games in New York. They won the World Series in 1933 and

FIRST BASEMAN WILLIE McCOVEY

1954. But fans stopped coming to their games. In 1958, the Giants moved to San Francisco.

San Francisco fans loved the Giants. The team was often near the top of the **STANDINGS**. The Giants played in the World Series three times but lost. Finally, in 2010, they won a world championship for San Francisco. Two years later, they won another!

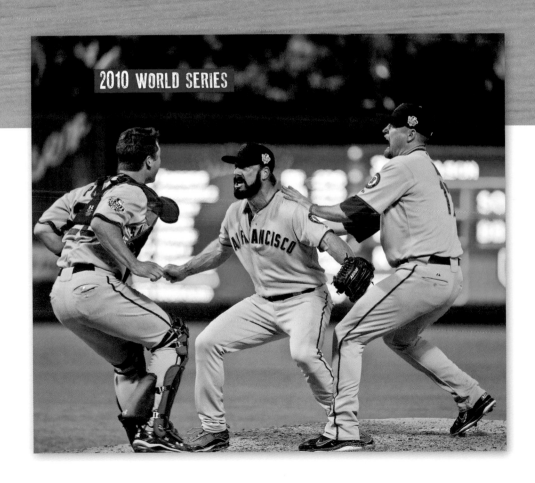

2010 WORLD SERIES

WILLIE MAYS

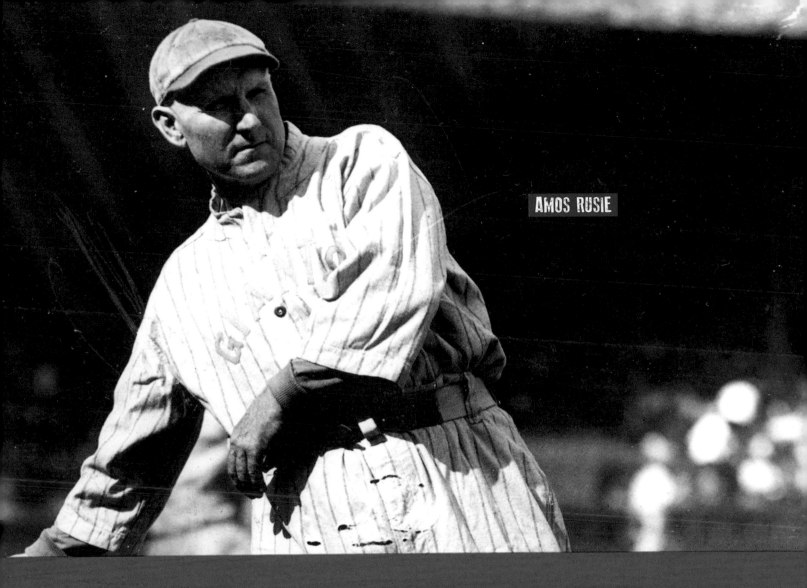

AMOS RUSIE

GIANTS STARS

Amos Rusie was a star pitcher who won 234 games for the Giants in the 1890s. In 1951, Willie Mays joined the Giants. His big hits and amazing catches in center field made him a superstar.

In 1993, the Giants signed slugging outfielder Barry Bonds. He

set a major-league **RECORD** for **CAREER** home runs. Pitcher Tim Lincecum also set records in San Francisco by striking out a lot of batters.

In 2009, catcher Buster Posey joined the Giants. His great hitting and strong throwing helped San Francisco win the World Series in 2010 and 2012. Fans hoped Posey would help the Giants capture more championships soon!

BUSTER POSEY

TIM LINCECUM

SF 0 B3 s 2 o 0

BARRY BONDS

HOW THE GIANTS GOT THEIR NAME

Until 1885, the Giants were called the Gothams. But after a great win that year, the team's manager was very proud of his players. He called them "My big fellows! My giants!" Sportswriters started calling the team the Giants, and the name stuck!

ABOUT THE GIANTS

First season: 1883

League/division: National League, West Division

World Series championships:

1905	*4 games to 1 versus Philadelphia Athletics*
1921	*5 games to 3 versus New York Yankees*
1922	*4 games to 0 versus New York Yankees*
1933	*4 games to 1 versus Washington Senators*
1954	*4 games to 0 versus Cleveland Indians*
2010	*4 games to 1 versus Texas Rangers*
2012	*4 games to 0 versus Detroit Tigers*

Giants Web site for kids:

http://mlb.mlb.com/sf/fan_forum/kids_index.jsp

Club MLB:

http://web.clubmlb.com/index.html

GLOSSARY

CAREER — all the years a person spends doing a certain job

CROSSTOWN — describing something on the other side of town

RECORD — something that is the best or most ever

RIVALS — teams that play extra hard against each other

STANDINGS — the rankings of sports teams from best to worst; they show how many wins and losses a team has

INDEX

AT&T Park. 9

Bonds, Barry 19–20

Lincecum, Tim 20

Mathewson, Christy . . . 12, 15

Mays, Willie. 19

New York Gothams. . . . 12, 23

Ott, Mel 15

Posey, Buster. 20

records. 20

rivals 10, 15

Rusie, Amos. 19

team colors 10

team name 12, 23

World Series. 10, 12, 15, 17, 20, 23